Freedom is fine Reed on money

Freeze domain

Jim Rana
Vasanta Madhavi
C Rajgopalachary

Some start

- Competition aligns with random sentiments and all rivals address full need of Customer together but not as sole final opponent in the best scene.
- Freedom of Customer is to be provided by a solid solution or cause for companies with freedom in business globally for new change.

Money

- Gives freedom of business with distinct risk of experiments in innovation but agile Companies can buy money instead of freedom that goes into management and change according to need and use of business offering.

Domain

- Constant exhaustion of attempts to understand Customer correctly and satisfying is freedom from competitor imitation
- Domain is customer, freeze domain to get new knowledge, products, cooperation and accountability freely.

Financial Reed

- Find Reed
- First Reed is in finance
- Fine Reed is in business etiquette
- Rein in business globally to refine Reed of Customer orientation
- Refine Reed of innovation
- Refund Reed of trust
- Reed is need redefined

What is Reed?

- Reed is business tree and that grows in blue water of Customer
- Reed is a good sound of common need of Customer as end of journey of inspiration if you fail to understand.

Reed is weed if

- The business offering gets away from the first need of Customer after different types of user perspective understanding exercise means that explore the blue ocean water in shallow depth or disturb Customer notion of need.

Relevance of freedom

- Business is better bound by Customer commitment than free
- Customer freed from purchase contract and agreement is better than greed of business trashed by Customer

Fine freedom

- Ability to bear unreasonable request from Customer is real business, that keeps you really busy or bus in essence of success, not money is counted like business endgame

Refine freedom

- Higher freedom is not informed thought and action free from biases only but also a whole domination of business ethics far from competitive fears
- The winner of strategic innovation beyond time is party with freedom.

Train like reign

- Whether you're employee or vendor or customer service experience is a common mission for new skill, knowledge, results procured from personal or professional network but we need a good attempt to understand what, how, why with a solid base of training in business etiquette, usage guidelines, of mastering the global solutions.

Tied losses

- Profits are free, losses tied to ignorance and stupidity
- Skills are used to step free, imitation ties to box
- Innovation is unboxed, renovation is tied to old
- Worries and failures are free property, parties and highs are tied to (be)cause and (side)-effect

In business freedom

- Interdependence is lost, this avoids mutual growth enrichment of department consideration, user interface with the right knowledge and existence of business changes with skills and experience.

Growing free

- Free your business of monetary greed
- Free your employees of lengthy process hurdles
- Free your customers of 'this is not in rules, we are checking again'
- Free your competition of business espionage

Stagnating free

- Lack of multilateral Strategy implementation could saturate a company growth prospects if you can not decide on what and how priority, one from the free opportunities many putting you at risk with competitors or Customers.

Growing free

- Business is better to challenge employees to think free, talk free, work free, fail free and win free from biases, fears and bureaucracy.
- Business is designed to allow for Customers to tell company what's wrong to grow free because if Customers are not free from restrictions your business success doesn't come for free.

Selling free

- Stores sell for free at festive season of exciting Customers with exchange of happiness of grabbing a product after a long queue wait to see future loyalty of Customer to pay for motivation of company initiatives in customer management.

Freedom is needed

- Technology and IP adoption should be hassle free
- Employers should have easy work terms with customers and employees
- Customer should have freedom so to say lie
- Business stakeholders should have clear freedom of Customer case resolution then and there.

Freedom models

- Bureaucracy is far.
- Flexible organisation structure is free to invent.
- Hierarchy defeats freedom of àgility.
- Employees are easy to convince for alternative solutions in firms following freedom model.
- Freedom model is entity's success of business working with customers with freedom.

Model has

- Freedom to choose cost effective methods, technologies and tools
- Freedom of information or direct feedback analysis
- Freedom of employee contribution
- Freedom to access your business heads
- Freedom to choose from different directions to fulfill expansion goals.

What should be free in company?

- Employees but not employment
- Consumer but not consumption
- Investment but not return
- Competition but not retaliation
- Utility but not resources behind the offering
- Testing but not resting
- Product but not issues

Freedom Constraints

- Employees are biased and bound by concerns of dependents
- Decision making and activities planning can never be as quick as attempted
- Product is most likely to get balanced between customers and employees

Bring change

- To get product innovation freedom
- To appreciate productivity of freedom
- To understand efficiency of business changes
- To utilisation of freedom to beat challenges
- To challenge the best
- To test the global network of users with different stakeholders', trust, confidence and dependence.

Bound by

- Demand of user sealed in personalized needs can not let your business entity free
- Political chaos and business changes, Customer is audience of unexpected expectations in own advancements and never free from biases.

Lead free

- Free employees are innovating and serving customers more than process bound ones
- Free Customers could forget company mistakes better than those taken to ride
- Free economy knows how to get new avenues of growth with other countries.

Dread free

- Customer should be free to communicate different frustrating feelings with business
- Employees should be free to give wild ideas to senior management
- Competition should be free to invent new and weird things for waste or haste to customer.

Crofty gimmick

- Leaders should look forward and plan higher than winners who look down but execute on Customer plans into making them the right leader who the best business leaders should look at, to get your business seem like a customer place.

Intelligent solutions

- That could walk with customers and employees
- That confirm duplicate demand of Customer
- That can work on decision on behalf of Customer in her favor
- That act as user champion in business globally.

Freedom's duration

- Lasts as long as a single employee fighting for fearless competition response for companies
- Is as much as early product success with customers until snatched by internal failure
- Can't wait for measuring but meaning which company can apply for Customer importance.

Freedom defies

- One condition is applicable to freedom and that is fearless competition in offering more than rivals to working with customers for providing specific but acceptable product
- There is no place for questioning employees but train them on your business methods for adjusting with broad corporate policy, unlike nations where freedom is unconditional.

Free Customer from

- Depending on human employee mood
- The chaos in market players
- Decision- limiting factor of your business products or services
- Influence of technology and market change.

Help customers with

- Free information management and business development data
- Freedom of communication
- Free business health feedback
- Free statistics of competition
- Real time market signals interpretation

Have some free

- Resources for further opportunity assessment
- Information for your rival food for new response
- Higher maintenance as gift for Customer loyalty
- Knowledge sources to be in open order of business need management
- Supply to get new demand fostered

Idea to solution

- Company travels through business flows, resource planning, Customer integration into business changes and not some direct procure-sell chain of deal management with customers as business is misinterpreted in buy-sell alone but some extra knowledge and value are also processed.

Stagnate free

- Industry expansion should benefit all players but stagnant industry could give good blow to big leader so Companies should challenge market for showing alternative opportunities for connecting other forms of growth and change.

Catching that free resource

- Such business gaps should be utilised by investment in research, Customer knowledge and technology training of not losing low-cost or free resources to yield results in all walks of business.

Free usage

- The customer and business are not free until they get new products that are free to use from your side of business changes and buyer adjustments, not zero price

Free terms

- Don't bind Customer in business terms
- Don't tie trust with price or other things but loyalty of Customer
- Have a set of terms and conditions but not without incremental consent of Customer in different gains

Freed technology

- Use technology but not without incremental backup of your employee teams to free technologies and tools of adopting Customer as smart solutions driver then freed technology is serviced by Customer who is a good learner to value your intelligence and not dependent upon technologies.

Deriving drivers

- Ask Customer to tell what they want from business centric process improvement
- Talk to customers and know how they buy or sell or make decisions
- Use technology to analyse the driver to get new facets of business changes.

Research

- Should be free to invent new and unconventional even weirder ideas for growth of employees, selling new products that are decent but evaluated by the public for convenience at community cause of learning.

Unconditional offer

- The changes in culture of business challenge employees to get unconditional in customer service and product promotion to understand Customer correctly for addressing all networks with maximum relevance of freedom to beat your competitors without condition of business loss to be giver of Customer.

User repartees

- You are not the only sellers on the market and Customer is not dependent on your favour
- Industry expansion is not Customer's need but your business'
- Standard quality assurance is not differentiator but one of prerequisites of players in the market.

Product details

- Current customers and market analysts are saying yes of business products in adapting their attributes of the community relevance to buyer as a fulfillment by guidelines associating user in the process and task of production making business leadership advantageous for stakeholders and technology excellence.

Strategic base

- The market and company changes could not be managed well without any strong and Strategic research background to your business foundation for industry growth

Limiting

- Factors of success to customer value, your business credibility or market intelligence can grow an appreciable success without creating a difference between customers and employees.

Free from trouble

- Customer should not feel that they bought trouble with the product
- Employees should not think that they will run on trouble for troubleshooting business

Free opportunities

- Innovation should be free from hidden interest better serving long term loyalty of Customer in future extension to social cause bringing corrections of business and markets in the best methods taking new shape of Customer needs

Customer experience

- Should be free from responsibility that is for employees to maintain accountable work ethics
- Should be free from contingency and research binding to get uninterrupted flow from needs to product

Product innovation must

- Have design gaps that are not facilitated but automatically generated in future Business offerings discovery
- Brand Innovation in accepting through your customer request for customisation of brand and branding customisation efforts in return.

Locus in focus

- Customer is focus of business value and business products or services rather remain to be locus for new change initiatives to a maximum growth by combining resources, market signals, competitive response and business research in direction of community service.

Methods are free

- Different types of ideas on ways to get the implementation success and business output of research by allowing use of resources can bring out better discretion of business decisions in handling their perceptions and administrative needs of Customer and employees as left free from restrictions.

Utility àgility

- The market teaches us to have àgility of business utilisation as resources are not wasted on corrections as desired mode of growth with leadership sidelined for new change initiatives in product innovation and excellence.

Opportunity for free

- The market growth and business changes seek user interface with employee commitment including social accountability in accepting the opportunities for free exploitation by investment of different types of resources.

Taste of tactics

- Current customers and business representatives are available for different feedbacks and ideas on how to use machine for making products but something different must be done in market for a course backwards to read products in adapting machine for next dawn of Innovation.

Customer is

- Closed book but we need to work with opening up new ways of improving their understanding, clarity or poise with the global business products or services in enabling them build expectations in demanding Innovative product from your business.

Series or other use

- Utility can grow or promote new ideas for technology innovation from one to another progression in the upgrading series or version on the path of utilisation of capabilities and output.

Systems analysis

- When machines analyse user data trends and preferences emerge
- When data scientist grills machine data new ideas for learning technologies can be derived by advanced brain interaction with intuitive intelligence.

Influence on technology

- Technology information on enhancing physical performance of the process and machines resulting in better product is most powerful if information technology is no longer affiliated to the personal preferences of management teams.

Customer cannot grow

- With users struggling for new business opportunity for your skill application in the process of growing employees by ignoring Customer concerns towards building trust around new ideas for growth in personal space.

Collaborative environment

- Even while interacting and competing with rivals the company should show collaborative environment before parting ways on reasons of differentiation and business branding in restoring business partnership prospects.

Guts of competition

- Can be compared with feedback from Customer in business preparation of handling undecidable market or rival response for competitive strategy in business readiness for excellence by Customer care or solutions delivery.

Technology opinion

- Review competitor or Customer participation in the global market solutions that are decent pointers to Technological inclinations that credit the system's utilisation in tweaking the market and user view of turnkey change Technology offering comfort of change management.

Refinement is not free

- Knowledge and skills refinements come by Technology and product innovation in promoting business identity and research to send rivals struggling with customers only to fail for references on technology innovations.

Challenges give

- Free opportunity for important learning and development of business products in adapting to customer side of need satisfaction by defeating competition in reducing tactics of redundant dependency on the market factors.

Capabilities unlocked

- Review competitor responses to reveal employee tendency for reversal of capability doubts or questions in the process of establishing innovation with learning as futuristic growth door.

Culture unraveling

- Current customers don't have a good attempt to get new impact without stopping by culture based adaptation to new solution management and technology alignment with scale and quality needs of global user network.

Boggling statistics

- One patent can get outdated in as less time as less than six months
- One successful completion of business solution can grow you atleast two new products
- Market research is more meaningless than a bookish theory.

General approach

- Custom your business through safeguarding your customer views for providing employee value of ideas and outputs to improve upon market power of creation of innovative solutions for cultural growth by small leaps.

Business problems

- Innovation and value addition
- Change and cultural preserving solutions
- Best efficiency and turnover
- Involvement of Employees and customers

Business eviction

- Exit what is needed by Customer when Customer does not use it
- Quit business when Customer doesn't need what employees do
- Leave product not uptrending with customers.

Betting market

- The market power comes from Customer-company bets on whether or not you as market gets some extra leverage of competitive strategy spread across industries, nations and world.

Up with your customer

- Organization's inertia can go away by timing Strategic response along Customers
- Company should be balanced and agile enough to send negative signals to rivals for new business movement in customer direction.

High volatilities

- Resources change performance, effort, efficiency, effectiveness, quality, goals, utilisation aspects, turnover to pick up with each market signal as preparation of business with customers in terms and conditions imposed by volatilities.

Current mission

- To connect in the business stakeholders
- To ignore competitors for uniqueness
- To reduce human errors or risk

We're the market users

- Business entities use market information on applying tools for fulfillment of desires of Customer in competing through a circuitous route for new change strategies addressing on your assessment of the market signals.

Cultural freedom

- Customer is in future duty of dynamic cultural cultivation and business developments could close out with the cultural freedom to choose cost of natural progression as a business strategy by controlling technology.

Defined by

- Customer, freedom is a common space in innovative solutions that can accommodate your unworthy demands
- Company, freedom is needed in business globally to refine understanding that usually takes to Innovation for satisfaction of Customer.

Time Customer

- Don't interact with customers at the cost of interruption in business or their time
- Give trust as a binding fact to understand what Customers want and what you would sell in the process of establishing superiority of Customer on business.

Leave rejection of mistake

- Accept Customer mistake as your responsibility in learning to work with your own
- Don't deny mistakes and trust together with false supremacy as dependency on Customers

Unused freedom

- Employees should train efficiency with optimising their own talent exploitation to get new results from new or existing business tasks by allowing change within skills and techniques of application increasing Customer delight.

Business is free economy

- Industry grows insight into what user expectations are and should be with balance on independence and responsibilities to get the right values and growth of employees contributing to that of Customers and economy.

User defined

- Boundaries of systems
- Functions of business solutions
- Need of Customer
- Can free your employees from Customer difference when above are defined by user.

User stories

- Should be able to pull more information on simple effective solution for betterment of business drivers besides synergistic utilisation of capabilities for the continued Innovative product creation.

Look at

- Competition to discover your business setbacks
- Market to account for your business credibility
- Customers to get new pointers on future business changes
- Employees to maintain logic behind your business culture.

Use

- Competitive imitation in saving business resources for further new business solution Innovation and challenges resolution on the path of utilisation of capabilities for stakeholder goal attainment.

A half

- Gain on Customer worth is not less than a free full grown victory over global competitors
- Baked Strategy is not worse than no backed understanding that is formless without Customer participation

Busting

- Machines are ruined by rough usage and disruption of business process
- Technology is futile in conditions of Customer not responding to its use and not accepting its culture of service automation.

Cultural differences

- Culture of Customer is trust
- Culture of business is designed with knowledge of customer
- Culture of technology is automating services
- Culture of employees stands on integrity against competitors till hired by them.

Do

- Consult your customers more than your business advisor on the market state of products that are facilitated for use of existing or new customer needs to get unknown technology included in the solution as advised by the experts.

Customers

- Are no free from biases, fears and resistance of another customer, family member or friend
- Can never be completely free from influence of competition or Technology variations levying apprehension on Customer ways of doing everything better or worse than others.

If icon

- Technology embodiment in the business solutions can grow iconic Innovation if Customer could be given more important role in the same getting treated as icon for new business opportunity identification.

Modern model

- Bases decision on strategic usage and adaptation by Customer
- Support attitude towards collective competition as change for good Customer service
- Leads Customer as market champion in driving innovation.

Innovative

- Mistakes are made by enthusiastic employees yearning to get new ideas reviving Customer delight
- Technology is equipped with your business credibility automated to get multiple things achieved by different users.

Mealing in

- Business output and offering is not just a cheap product, it's a great meal for consumer psyche to experiment with different ways of doing daily activities, in the process of getting old ideas replaced by advanced new requirement of the ages.

Structure adaptation

- Organisational skills and experience are not independent of automation but some extra flexible structures in the inclusion of growth inclinations to various segments of customers can get better business change.

Value of

- Business comes from Customer
- Customer comes from culture
- Culture comes from global network
- Global market comes from competition
- Competition comes from community.

Dependency on

- Time gives you scope for differentiation by value of the company offering worth Customer satisfaction or value of quality usage experience altered in cultural interest of international integration of community service.

Pullout Innovation

- Future business models or organisational frameworks should have clear freedom to get multiple Innovative product offerings pulled off from the beginning itself when Customer needs are identified.

Universal uniqueness

- Every company and product can get unique to address every customer in unique value of business global limelight in Innovation becoming the way of business with future.

Gratitude

Thanking your payment of attention to content, any mistake is author responsibility.

www.ingramcontent.com/pod-product-compliance
Lightning Source LLC
Chambersburg PA
CBHW020553220526
45463CB00006B/2288